Praise for James Brown

'*New Days for Old* is enchanting.'
—Jasmine Sargent

'James Brown is I think the funniest poet in this country. He's beautifully in control of tone and emotional power, so the poems sometimes just sneak up on you.'
—Damien Wilkins, RNZ

'Hilariously clever: a linguistic and intellectual delight.'
—Margaret Austin, *Regional News*

'Of all Palmerston North's Creative Giants, poet and short fiction writer James Brown stands out . . .'
—Palmerston North Creative Giants

'The James Brown of New Zealand poetry.'
—Dr Ernest M. Bluespire

Also by James Brown

Go Round Power Please (1995)
Lemon (1999)
Favourite Monsters (2002)
The Year of the Bicycle (2006)
Warm Auditorium (2012)
Floods Another Chamber (2017)
Selected Poems (2020)
The Tip Shop (2022)
Slim Volume (2024)

New Days for Old

James Brown

Te Herenga Waka University Press
Victoria University of Wellington
PO Box 600 Wellington
teherengawakapress.co.nz

First published 2026

A catalogue record is available at the National Library of New Zealand.

ISBN 9781776923052

Printed in China through Asia Pacific Offset

Much of the greatest art, I find, seeks to remind us of the obvious.

—Patrick Bringley, *All the Beauty in the World: A Museum Guard's Adventures in Life, Loss and Art*

In my country of origin, far across the sea, the women sweep the floors with what you would call broomsticks. These are effective until their ends begin to fray and snap, creating more debris than they clean away. This was also the problem with our government, which is why my father disguised us as suitcases and brought us here.

People's natures on display everywhere you turn. Looking around, your eyes meet heads bowed to phones. You can't wait to be given one, but in the meantime demand the pierced nipple lactate into *your* mouth. Outside, a bumper sticker shouts *Burn Coal – Drive Electric*. This makes you want to crawl away and cry, which, when released, you do because, at 8 months old, you hear whatever you do is 'very advanced'.

A life that only comes into being as you type it, stuttering footsteps in an alley. ‘Someone’s a drunken fool,’ says your uncle.

Legoland was a safe place for a child to play. My mother was a pepper pot. My father wielded a circular saw. I rode a train of thought through tunnels and a small quarry town to the same station I'd left. If the economy were better, I could earn more money, buy more rails and make my own way in the world, I mean, make the world in my own way, I mean, own the world.

We take lasagna round to John because 'He's fallen through the cracks,' says my mother. That must be why it's bad luck to step on them. 'The trickle-down theory is a plate of pish-posh,' she adds. When we arrive, John is sword fighting the air with a cake fork.

My father located my slow puncture, rotating the tube in the sink until a fine line of bubbles appeared. 'Difficult to detect,' he said, marking it. 'Like dark matter. There. Jesus wants me for a sunbeam.'

I lie down on the footpath to examine the textures in the concrete. This sinkhole would suit a game of marbles. Aunt Esme has a jar of marbles on her mantelpiece because 'They're beautiful – like glass eyes'. At school, we learn about the eye-of-God perspective. When I show Aunt Esme my *Book of the Planets*, she calls Neptune 'the prettiest marble in our solar system'. I fit my finger into the sinkhole and hang on.

Leone's best friend Alice lived in a thimble Leone kept hidden under her pillow. One day she came home and saw her mother darning socks, the thimble bobbing like a finger puppet. Her mother tried to reassure her that Alice was fine, that Alice had left the thimble and gone out for a walk. But Alice was not fine and had not gone out for a walk. Leone went into their room and looked out the window. She would learn to play the violin because that was the only way Alice or the sky could be spoken of.

Our family meals were scripted. 'What the dickens is going on?' demanded Father, marching his toast soldiers into his poached egg. 'Will you not slaughter a pig, Mother?' He raised his fork to us like a conductor. 'Whatever happened to the crispy bacon we used to have before the war?' we chorused. '*Twenty-one years in cap-tivi-ty,*' he sang. '*Shoes too small to fit his feet,*' we responded. Our mother sighed and promised to let us eat cake.

By candlelight, you were almost a rational number. Your pencil stub threw shapes across the page. Your voice, usually a mumble of feathers, suddenly seemed to articulate. 'Do you have something you'd like to share?' said Ms Poole with an e, who taught maths. You liked how she'd swung by your desk to help you with parabolas, but what was she doing in your bedroom? You read out your solution. Her Juicy Fruit breath explained where you'd gone wrong and blew out the candle.

We were testing the strength of our English teacher's patience. She cheerfully swatted away Byron's dart. She made Wordsworth come inside and Coleridge return to his seat. She even laughed at the anatomical drawing on Wollstonecraft's desk, calling it 'wistful'. And she seemed unfazed by the random chirping noises coming from the cupboard behind her desk, ignoring them until the end of class. But when she lifted the latch and found Hölderlin huddled inside, she turned to us with eyes blazing.

The grass verge our cricket wicket. The corner shops our CBD. The street lights our aurora. Bo Derek our standard bearer.

I hawk my tray of ice creams backstage at the Regent Theatre. Widow Twankey selects a Jelly Tip and raises her voluminous skirts in payment. 'Off you go now, you little scamp,' she says, blowing me an elaborate kiss.

My father gave me a smiley sticker saying *Kenny Ball and his Jazzmen*. I stuck it on a large moneybox tin with its smile as the slot. I deposited only 'snows' – our pet name for silver coins. The coins did seem to melt because no matter how heavy the tin got, it never reached capacity. For years I hauled it around different flats until one day I came home to a break-in. The tin was gone. This was to be the first of several break-ins. Each time, drawers would be turned out in search of money. But, unfortunately for all concerned, the snows had stopped falling.

The waves chased dogs up the sand. Aunty H removed her shoes, ashamed of what she called her gull's feet. Bags of dog poo sat on the sea wall waiting to be abandoned. There is standing room and much to be thankful for in the present. Look, a handstand on the beach.

A man, beached like a seal in foam, spoons his flippers through wet sand. Yoga lady salutes the sun. Bookmark woman prolongs a handstand, her landing strip perfectly balanced. On calm days, you can breaststroke through the rocky channel, following your shadow over sand and seaweed. Yes, it is idyllic, but one must return to one's towel and uniform.

A new microwave I'm trying to stack slips off the forklift. 'It doesn't matter if a few things fall over the side, so long as the ship sails on,' I tell my boss. 'Unless you're one of the things,' he says. 'Or we're all on the *Titanic*.'

It’s a shop that specialises in the unwanted. Out front sit trolleys of things they can’t give away. Inside, you wander through loose categorisation. You like the old glass bottles, thick and mottled like your grandmother’s forearms. What might they have contained? Elbow grease and ignorance? Sucked cheeks and shoe squeaks? Hiccups and tear ducts? Do we need to shake things up a little, the marble pushing against the rubber until a desirous finger relieves the pressure?

As a child, it was your grandmother's job to collect the eggs. She would walk nervously down the long driveway toward the henhouse, keeping an eye out for the magpie. In spring, it would plummet like a hawk from the lone poplar. Your grandmother ran for the cover of the hay barn as it whooshed her flossy hair. 'It's protecting its nest,' said her father, reluctant to shoot it. 'But we need the eggs,' said her mother.

I was a victim of circumstance. The wind funnelled through the streets. I saw whole families picked up and carried away. The Pembertons held hands like paper chain people. One day, I stopped fighting and let the wind take me too. That food bank was once a petrol station, which was once a field where my sister looked after a horse. Mostly she just brushed it and blew softly into its nose. Some horses like that.

‘It’s always darkest before the dawn,’ my father used to say. We were pit ponies, and stabled underground with oats and water. At dawn the men would arrive, blinding us with their headlamps before our eyes adjusted to the suns and shadows.

In the New Zealand edition of *Monopoly*, Old Kent Road has been replaced by Palmerston Street. In the Palmerston North edition, it's Linklater Reserve. My mum carries the one I found on Trade Me past the green plastic houses disowning Moheke Ave. She stops to show me where the free food stand, which had to be relocated, used to be. The corner house where the woman was murdered remains untenanted, while the semi-detached shot at in a drive-by and barely able to contain its anger is unlikely to win second prize in a beauty contest.

In The Alice, no one had seen the sea except Lawrence, who wasn't much given to conversation. In my mind, it was always bordered – like a paddock or pudding or Lawrence's watery eyes behind his glasses that didn't have any actual lenses in them. We were inlanders through and through. Our water came from bores. The movement of groundwater can be mathematically modelled if you know enough variables, thought Oscar Edward Meinzer, who didn't believe in thumb twiddling.

I'd never seen the dairy's door closed. Through a grimy pane, I saw *Tip Top* really had looked like *Jip Jop*. I could just about make out Mrs Lombard's lamington face. I tapped the window. Mrs Lombard gave a startled bleat and blundered out through a wormhole in the accounting into the abandoned garden.

To begin with, I often got an interview. On one occasion, the usual questions exhausted, the interviewers told me I was one of two people they were considering for the position, so what could I say to make them choose me over the other person. 'Well,' I said, thinking outside the box, 'if you give me their name and address, I'll go round and kill them.' They loved that – and I got the job! No, of course I didn't.

'Maybe you should make a business card,' Tony tells me, and gives me his.

The Valley of the Green Tears
Operations

Garden Maintenance   Exotic Firewood
Painting   Furniture Removals   Cat Rescue
Small Scale Demolition   Advice

TEL: (04) 970-3909
EMAIL: mcgruddy@excite.com

You were a semicolon in the last printed edition of the *Encyclopaedia Britannica*, which ran to 32 volumes. You provided a crucial pause between two connected but discrete ideas about the nature of being. But no one wants printed editions anymore. Editions before your time, back when everyone was pausing to consider things, might be sought after; you, however, have been hurried past and swing like a hook and eye between two seams coming apart.

Online shopping had transformed the High Street. Nail salons jostled with hairdressers where I set up my Biscuit Cart. No one could resist my ginger kisses. I admired the way the shop girls licked the cream from their manicured nails. 'They remind me of childhood,' said one. 'They remind me of body butter,' said another, retracting her claws. 'Break over, back inside,' said Madame Manicure, wagging her finger at me.

I moved to a town of dead umbrellas. Early each morning, I left my room and door-knocked. 'Nothing going here,' said the owl-faced receptionist, who would show me in for an official job interview the very next day. Thus, I became a Visual Display Artist. For decency, we covered the windows while we dressed the mannequins, holding the season's fashions to their ski-slope limbs with double-sided tape. We positioned open umbrellas as a backdrop while, outside, the wind shook the glass like an angry snowdome owner trying to make a point.

The sky was slippery and overlooked an inky lake. Long-distance swimmers hardly use their legs. 'I'm becoming half fish,' said one, pulling herself onto the jetty. 'Ironically,' I said, 'if you do develop a tail, it's your arms you'll hardly use.' 'Except for gestures and guidance,' she said, pooling in the sun and pointing me toward her banana.

Her pout as she applied Russian Red, the stick raised to her lips like a sliced finger, the little dog at her feet licking its aerial. The way she turned from the mirror and sipped from a glass of milk. Such dramas to bear witness to.

I glided through the days and weather and people as if covered in Johnson's Baby Oil. Nothing could stop me. So this was being in love. How wonderful. I wanted to snap my fingers.

A soft-voiced man in a brown suit speaks to Jesus's offer of salvation, his hands proffering pamphlets like doves. A young Greenpeace woman approaches with her clipboard. A man outside KFC claims he was once served Kentucky fried chaffinch. The Earth's rotation is caused by our footsteps. If enough people walk in one direction, they can turn the Earth toward them.

On the footpath, I find a small handwritten card.

James

– Wallmanning

Desperately Seeking Baby. Oh Baby Where Art Thou? Babyspotting. Hunt for the Wilderbabies. Heavenly Babies. Hidden Babies. Sleeping Babies. The Wicker Baby. A Clockwork Baby. Edward Babyhands. Butch Baby and the Sundance Kid. The Princess Baby. Kung Fu Baby. The Big Lebabeski. Babylon. The Incredibly Strange Creatures Who Stopped Living and Became Mixed-Up Babies. Dead Poets' Babies. Reservoir Babies. The Lost Babies. The Remains of the Baby. Baby to the Centre of the Earth.

Koha entry at the Newtown Community Centre. Janice on sound, the thin crowd glad to escape the cold. Janice taps the mic. 'RON57. You've left your lights on.'

Is your carnival complete, Mr Daniel Levy, because my eyes need a rest? They didn't touch the ground from goal kick to Hoddle's net-bound volley or when Ricky Villa turned Man City into practice cones or the Welsh Wizard flew past Inter Milan. After seeing the movie *Escape to Victory*, I practised Ossie Ardiles' rainbow flick over and over, though it's of no practical use, even on a football field.

We were party balloons bonded by shared breath. As the night wore on, some of us broke free to bump together on the ceiling. 'I love you.' 'No, I love you.' Next morning, the aunties arrived to tidy and vaccuum. Organising Aunty opened doors and windows and moved us on. I was placed in the care of a boy in a pushchair eating a piece of chalk.

‘James, come quick, the Winstanley Building’s being demolished.’ From the fire escape, we watched the first ball swing. ‘Good,’ I said. Susan, who knew what fanlights were, made a small plughole noise like our drain before it blocked.

Yes, he had once removed all his clothes and played naked, because, he said, if you play the cello, it just seems like something you ought to do.

Back to the Baby. It's a Baby, Baby, Baby, Baby World. It's a Wonderful Baby. The Godbaby. Casababy. Jurassic Baby. Apocalypse Baby. Moonrise Baby. One Baby After Another. There's Something About Baby. Babyheimer. Babyrella. Baby and Babier. The Baby of Oz. The Quiet Baby. One Flew Over the Baby's Nest. The Boy in the Baby Pyjamas. Conan the Babyrian. Babies by Numbers. Babies in the Mist. The Silence of the Babies. 20,000 Babies Under the Sea.

Magnificently awful, the moths battering against the dark pane in which you see a pale version of yourself. Hello, lost soul song hovering in darkness. Unlike the moths, you don't seem to want to come in.

Being able to fly wasn't all you'd hoped. You couldn't flit about town in the day without becoming a research subject, which meant flying mostly at night. Flying long distances was cold, and still took hours. You couldn't go at Superman speed because breathing became impossible, like sticking your head out a fast-moving car. You had to wear goggles and weatherproof clothing and carry a change of clothes in a backpack. Navigation was tricky, especially over water. It was easier to take a plane.

The power of invisibility? Easy. Hop on a bicycle and suddenly no one can see you. Cycle clips betray deep-cover spies, fixies are the steed of choice for faceless hackers and coders, and, to the side of every foreground, the anonymous poor treadle their clunkers. Even as we whisper to one another now, the can-and-bottle boy is pushing his Frankenbike home from the dumpster. Lean closer. Even God uses a bicycle to keep an eye on our little secrets. That exercycle in your bedroom – maybe move it.

The small town was as quiet as its museum. I walked the rows of stuffed birds like a general inspecting his troops, each one fixing me with an angry glass stare. In the Indigenous Room, everything was carved or woven. In the Settler Room, everything was tarnished. 'Makes you think, doesn't it?' said the proprietor, come to tell me they closed between 12 and 2 for counter lunch over the road.

The rock wall is a hive of activity. Flowers offer their wares to butterflies and bees, a spider waddles for a crack, while lines of ants connect the dots. Above it all tocks the pendulous tail of a cat watching a skink. The artist seems to have captured everything in oil but, the closer you get, the more it becomes a lumpy Dr Seuss landscape you want to touch your finger to. The cat's tail, too, has paused.

Our Daphne isn't happy. Some Daphnes have high tolerance levels, but ours detests wet feet and doesn't take kindly to bouts of wind. Relocation led to sulking and a withdrawal of the heady, beguiling fragrance we'd loved walking into. At a time when most Daphnes were flourishing delicate bouquets, ours offered bare limbs. We remove our hats and stand awkwardly. You were temperamental, Daphne, but we're sorry we failed to address your concerns. We miss your mischievous scents of humour and modest mauve smiles. Please don't leave us.

The old upright lived outside under the wattle tree. It was hopelessly out of tune, but the sight of her struggling with John Cage in her lavalava more than made up for the unprepared piano.

Carry On Baby. Around the World in 80 Babies. Baby Story. Even Babies Started Small. Little Miss Baby. Babyfinger. The Man with the Golden Baby. I Was a Teenage Baby. I Was a Baby for the FBI. The Baby from Another Planet. Baby 13. Tinker Tailor Soldier Baby. *Les Bébés Dangereuses*. Beyond the Valley of the Babies. They Shoot Babies Don't They? Saving Baby Ryan. The Baby Horror Baby Show. The Baby's Speech. Baby-Proof Fence. Baby Without a Cause. Baby and Me.

The time of near enough is almost here. Goodbye perfect pencils, flawless features, names in lights. Welcome you who tripped coming into the room. Take a seat among us. What have you forgotten to bring to share?

Another freezing evening for pottery class. I'd thought I was signing up for poetry – a common mistake. We bent over our wheels trying to centre our clay. The instruction was to 'make your idea of God'. I'd brought coloured beads and bottle caps as accessories. The woman opposite me sat before her wheel with eyes closed. I wanted to use her eyelashes, which couldn't be real but were. 'God loves a try-hard,' murmured the woman to my right, who often talked to herself.

Life had been good to them. The health system had kept them healthy. The land's resources had continued to tease the economy. Their country had avoided wars and they had avoided taxes. Sometimes their team didn't win or someone upset someone else, but these things were, as they themselves would tell you, not important in the grand scheme of things.

It was the summer of cloud. Two girls sat on the sea wall in transparent raincapes like goldfish in plastic bags. They licked their ice creams in the drizzle. One by one, the passing ferries were cancelled or sank. 'Outrageous,' said a seagull. 'Richard David Bach is a terrible writer.'

Powertool men, powertool men, let the sanding stop and the painting begin.

Forget stadiums and enormous outdoor festivals. Who doesn't want to play to an audience of friends in a café run by your neighbour's mother? 'I like a boogie,' she says as she shimmies her way between the tables and solo dads. It's a sellout. Even James the pug has snuck himself in. Only her daughter stares blankly from behind the counter. She isn't going to turn the espresso machine off just because it's a quiet song.

The man in the street.
The woman in absentia.
The elephant in the ointment.

A woman with a red hat gets on the bus at a stop
nobody gets on at. *Aah dee doo, ah dee doo dah day.*
A woman and child exit the bus at a bookmark in the
middle of the middle volume of *In Search of Lost Time*.
Read Proust for soft focus. *Aah dee doo, ah de daay dee.*
A lamp post on a windy hillside recedes into gorse and
bedstraw.

Her hands were so cold.

The 30X route ended at a bus shelter stuck like a stamp on the wrong corner of an envelope that had passed through several time zones. There was water damage along one edge, which was torn in places, revealing what looked to be a lock of hair. Water had also flooded part of the address, turning the cursive into a tideline of footprints. These were Mollie's or Millie's or Nellie's, but which number did she live at? The driver and postie were trying to make this out.

A house in a quiet suburb you used to visit regularly. You even walked fascinating circuits around its street-adjacent streets. Past the former petrol station, once known for its easy WOFs. Past Masie Jayne's, the corner shop kept afloat by vapes. Past Hairfalutin, with its fairy lights and family fights. Everything a-shimmer, especially her words, because they came from her mouth and went into yours, mixing your metaphors, until one day you both woke up at the end of the section.

The beach speckled in summer snow. I walk the tideline pecking at the polystyrene globules. A couple of other broilers strut past clucking and tutting. 'Rubbish,' we agree. Every high tide, all our little chickens come home to roost.

Amy removed her glasses and used a lens to compress the sun to a white dot on the paper. She held it to one spot. 'It always takes longer than you think.' How different she looked without her glasses. Snorkmaiden in *Moominsummer Madness*. Tove Jansson spent summers on a tiny island. The whiteness of the dot began to bleach my retinas. Then it darkened and a wisp of smoke appeared. The paper started to smoulder. Amy held the focus and we had ignition. She lifted the flaming pages and turned toward the pile of books.

The sandflies came from my lost decade. We stood topless on a lonely Fiordland shore seeing who could withstand them the longest. Neither of us was going anywhere.

Not Another Baby Movie. The NeverEnding Baby. The Big Baby. They Might Be Babies. There Will Be Babies. Star Babies. Pulp Babies. Inglorious Babies. 12 Angry Babies. Babies of the Lost Ark. Night of the Living Babies. The Lord of the Babies. The Good, the Bad, and the Baby. Close Encounters of the Third Baby. Four Babies and a Funeral. Brave New Baby. Citizen Baby. Saturday Night Baby. Baby of Arabia. Dr Strangebabe. Eternal Sunshine of the Spotless Baby. Singing in the Baby. The Last Baby. Run Baby Run.

A mirror is a friend who doesn't always say the right thing. Most people want friends they can trust. Please be honest, they say. Look me in the eye and say that, says the mirror.

Excuse me? It's not getting hotter, it's just another beautiful day. You should go to the beach. Pile the kids and dog in the car. Take a flight to Fiji. Hire a jet-ski. Do one of those walks – the Kimono Way. Experiencing new places and cultures fosters empathy and broadens the mind. Excuse me, can I get past you? Thanks. Excuse me – coming through. Excuse me.

‘I am sorry to learn that the accent falls on the middle syllable of Orakau. So much the worse for an impractical word – *quad versu dicere non est.*’

William Hodgson (1826–94)

He was full of good ideas. One was that a big concert be held with performers from everywhere. The world would unite through music, bringing an end to intolerance and hostility. Another was that the unemployed be utilised to dig a large lake that people could use for recreation. The excavated earth would be placed immediately beside the lake and sculpted to form a mountain, which would also provide recreational opportunities. He was particularly pleased by the synergy of this.

‘The Devil walks among us,’ says the man at my door. The devils I know never walk anywhere because they have too much to do. A skeleton staff and still the cuts keep coming. How can evil hold its own in a world overflowing with benevolent gods? The man talks about my footprints and God carrying me. I consider this. Indeed, something hath raised me from my bed and carried me down the hall to answer the door, my horns besmirched by hope.

Our drain would block every few years. Around that time, I was reading things like *living in the / universe doesn't / leave you / any place to chuck / stuff off / of.* 'Pōhutukawa keep us in business,' says Marty, lowing in the snake. 'They're not native to Wellington,' he tells me. 'Righto Sean. Turn it on.' And listening to things like *One of us is a cigar stand / and one of us is / a lovely blue incandescent guillotine.* 'Okay Sean, off.' And writing things like *What I like about rain / is its gravity.* 'You want the warthog, Mart?' 'Yeah, bring the warthog.' Or was that the previous winter?

After incinerating the witch, Gretel became a firefighter. Hansel, however, drifted about, getting skinnier and skinnier, eventually becoming the village idiot, a position I'd vacated when elected to council. It was a natural progression, but one I deeply regretted. Hansel often found me sobbing in the square. He suggested the council employ a town crier, a job he said I was better suited for. Gretel left the fire service and now works for Save the Children.

Sand between your toes as you walk to work in a town far from the sea. You sit on a park bench to remove your shoe. Sand pours out. A child runs over from the swings with a bucket and spade. More children come over. The sand flows down to a pond where sudden waves wash in beneath expectant, circling gulls. Mothers gather, kicking off their loafers. You cradle your foot as if it were a strange sea creature, brushing away flecks before guiding it carefully back into a sock in need of darning, then into your shoe, its tongue lolling, which you lace lazy-tight with a turquoise turtle knot before continuing on to work.

Diva Tessa saw Anna was asset-avid. Grammar and symmetry, their parents counselled, industry and thrift. For every dropped stitch you saved nine. There's no such thing as too many sequins.

The new class was gathered in a long room with tiered seating on both sides. Some students were wearing school uniforms. I explained that you couldn't just turn up, that you had to apply. The uniform group got up and left, leaving the successful applicants. I recognised one from last year, who sat apart, looking out at the trees. 'Hello Kerry,' I said. 'Terry,' the student said. 'Sorry Terry,' I repeated, writing it down. 'Is that with a Y or an I?' 'T–E–A–R–R–E–Y.' 'And what surname would you like me to use?' I turned to the rest of the class, who were looking uncertain, and said, 'This isn't a writing exercise. You don't have to make up a name. We just don't want to get on the wrong side of Admin.'

I once had a cup of tea with Stanley Fish and there was a storm in it. 'Good cooks can crack two eggs in one hand,' he said. We discussed a man pushing a shopping trolley with a parking meter in it. Was he collecting trolleys or meters? Or time? Stanley said this sounded like a thesis proposal he'd read – and laughed uproariously. The waitress, in her final year of something awful, shared a C+ smile with us.

A sunny, fierce-nosed kid with a double bass attached to his back. It watches over him at night while he sleeps in its case. Decades of night, triangles of night, night lines bending in and out of shape. 'Hey,' calls out a woman, 'didn't you used to be Charles Mingus?'

The days of yore were upon us. The first people they crushed were those who had learned from the past and not participated in its repetition. The days of yore did things a little differently, but we didn't become the foreign country foretold because their desired outcomes aligned with those we wished for ourselves. Praise be. Oh glorious spherical days! Oh beholden refracted epochs!

A key in a lock is a metaphor as old as Freud. We hid ours in a glove inside an outside drawer – the first place any burglar would look. Each time we let ourselves in, the door opened a little easier. Then gradually the grains, the tones, the stains started to disappear . . . until there wasn't a door at all. The mechanism's turn, alignment, click – gone. It wasn't stolen from us, we let it slip out.

Dubai floated on sand and oil. I was given a paintbrush and tins of 'mosque green' paint. My job was to work my way through the artificial trees in the glittering foyers and paint the gold leaves green. Elsewhere, a gilder worked reapplying gold leaf for autumn. For winter we replaced the leaves with strings of opals. Then spring and summer blossomed again beneath my brush, the leaves growing stronger and thicker with each passing season.

A blackboard choreographed in balletic proofs. The mathematician takes a step back. A murmur, then a cough. Somewhere in *Swan Lake*, a goose. The mathematician takes a second step back. Where did the chalk honk? Is that the price of fish?

They were a loquacious people. Even their ears could talk. I saw a small boy crouched in a corner covering his, trying to make them stop.

This isn't buying the baby a new dress. But we no longer have a baby. And in a box somewhere there's the sequinned pavlova of frills our old baby used to wear. As a toddler, he would twirl around the room with the lights off and a torch positioned just so. No music. I remember this at 3am when the room fills with moonlight.

Four in the morning and the night amplifies the wolves. The sky glows with stars. Maybe there is a creator? You can see why early cultures went down that route. You head down to the shore, hoping bioluminescence can occur in fresh water.

The people at the next table suggest that using the blind side could be the way to win. What a puzzling notion. 'Yes,' nods one, 'if our hooker gets a tighthead.' Goodness gracious. They see me staring at them. 'We're going to take you to the cleaners,' says one, jabbing his finger. Am I that odorous? I received my sponge bath only yesterday or possibly the day before yesterday.

The Hindenburg bird is so called because of its brightly coloured plumage. The monotony bird is so called because of its fondness for repeating the bell and butterfly haiku at every opportunity. The irony bird is so called because it is your good idea, the one you thought had legs, soaring out of sight.

‘Their arms were songs and their language a series of clicks.’ ‘Language? How do you know they were speaking?’ said George hotly. Dick ordered another margarita. ‘Maybe “language” is the wrong word.’ The lights flickered, then went out – common in this part of the world. Anne returned from backstage wearing a red-checked headscarf – her hilarious ‘basket of goodies’ impersonation. I knocked over Dick’s drink with my tail. ‘Come on everyone,’ said Julian, ‘I could eat a horse.’ ‘I could eat an elephant,’ said Dick. ‘I could eat Africa,’ said George. I was starving too, but I couldn’t eat Africa because all the animals and people there might not want to be eaten. They might feel we were taking advantage of them.

Money for jam, the advert said. I got the job. My supervisor gave me a glass jar and showed me to a hilltop. The hours were long – in fact, forever – but I enjoyed hunting for berries and filling the water-cooler from the well.

Notes

Page 5, epigraph: Patrick Bringley, *All the Beauty in the World: A Museum Guard's Adventures in Life, Loss and Art* (Random House, 2023), p. 22.

Page 15, 'Our family meals were scripted': The lines sung and responded to are from 'Free Nelson Mandela' by the Special AKA.

Page 21, 'The waves chased dogs up the sand': The penultimate line is also the penultimate line of 'A Dead Lamb' by Allen Curnow. The last line adapts his poem's last line.

Page 28, 'In the New Zealand edition of Monopoly': The New Zealand and Palmerston North Monopoly locations are genuine.

Page 55, French speakers will have noticed that *Les Bébés Dangereuses* should be *Les Bébés Dangereux*.

Page 63, 'A woman with a red hat gets on': *Aah dee doo, ah dee doo dah day* might be recognised by music buffs as the non-lexical vocables of 'The Gypsy Rover'. 'Read Proust for soft focus' is a line from 'XV. Randall Jarrell' by Dan Chiasson.

Page 73, 'I am sorry to learn': Taken from a footnote by William Hodgson to his poem 'Orakau', *The Poems of William Hodgson* (Alfred G. Betts, 1896), p. 65.

Page 76, 'Our drain would block': The first quote is from 'Pathway to the Sea' by Ian Wedde. The second is from 'Type Slowly' by Pavement. The third is from 'I Think One Last' by James Brown.

Page 79, 'Diva Tessa saw Anna was asset-avid': The last line is an abridged line from 'Concerning Some Recent Criticism of His Work' by Mark Doty.

Acknowledgements

Special thanks to Catherine, Ashleigh, and Fergus.

My thanks to Tony for allowing me to reproduce his business card (page 32).

Initial drafts of page 67 ('The beach speckled in summer snow') and page 78 ('Sand between your toes as you walk to work in a town far from the sea') were written in response to and published in the catalogue of . . . *a murmuring cave of the sea* . . . – an exhibition by Euan Macleod, Bowen Galleries, 2025. My thanks to Euan and to Greg O'Brien for generating this.

For the 'Baby' poems (pages 41, 47, 55, 70), my thanks to Zak for sharing his vast movie knowledge.

Page 11 ('We take lasagna round to John'), page 25 ('As a child, it was your grandmother's job'), and page 61 ('Forget stadiums and enormous outdoor festivals') first appeared in *Potluck: Poems about food* (Landing Press, 2025). My thanks to the editorial team.